A MYSTIC MARIONETTE

By

ARAVIND KRISHNAPPA RAO

DEDICATION

- To my beloved father **Venkatramana Krishnappa Rao.** You helped me to take that first single step. You gave me absolute freedom to self-examine myself, as, what can be done by me and what cannot be. Every, page of this book carries your soul. A rare gem you are.

- To my beloved mother **S.Thulasi Bai.** It is because of you I am here today. I am indebted to you till the end of my life.

- To my beloved better half **Nithya Gunasekaran alias Pattu.** You are kind-hearted, a honest crytic, a caring soul. A perfect motivator and you encourage me a lot. Immense to say about you. The book is all yours pattu.

- To my lovely daughters **Akshaya (a) Chinna, Ananya (a) Sonu, Saktipriya, Jagasri** four cherubs from the heaven, God's gift to us. I am learning everyday from you four and it is reflected in my writing. Long live you all, with the blessings of the Almighty.

ACKNOWLEDGEMENTS

- **Shivaram,** my inspirational friend, one who plays the fiddle of motivation at all the seasons and encourages me to the core to achieve my passion.

- **Ramesh Sriram,** my childhood friend, philosopher and guide. Your blessings will always follow as a shadow in my writing.

- **Ramanan Gururaj,** my cousin, an optimistic person, who always gives pat on my shoulders and utter 'you can do it at any cost'.

- **Vinotha,** my sister, one who showers positive vibes through her words of encouragement. One who gives prime importance to individuality a lot in a person. Thanks for your kind words.

COPYRIGHT NOTICE

PROLOGUE

My sincere benedictions to the almighty, our Guru Acharya Sri Raghavendrar Swamigal.

"Poojyaya Raghavendraya Sathya Dharma Rathayaksha Bhajatham Kalpa Vrikshaya Namatham Kaama Denavey". Honest prayers to my beloved Master OSHO.

I was put up in a seventh heaven with an unalloyed pleasure, when you all gave a huge response to my first e-book "coign of vantage". I bow my head humbly to you all, for a warm welcome given to the first child.

Once again, I knock all your doors with an invitation to read my second book "A mystic marionette."

Man has absolutely lost himself in the world of machines. He cares a jot for human emotions, moral and ethical values in this AI world. Bygone are the days, when he wakes up to the cry of cock-a-doodle-doo.

Today, phone alarm makes him alert. Laughter bursted between me and my cousin two months back when he visited my home. One fine morning, he woke up from his sleep and scolded me incessantly. Hey! Why you had not sent 'Good morning' message to me in WhatsApp today. Although it is ridiculous, truth is concealed behind this.

When the children build castles in the river sand, they rejoice in ultimate happiness. But it goes unnoticeable. A purest love floats in air, when a mother embraces her child and feed the child by pointing her fingers towards the beauty of moon. When it rains cats and dogs, kids in an exalted state fraternize with paper-boat and play with it in the rain water. De facto, it is a Noah's ark for them.

Man inherits certain attitudes and attributes by birth and it is his natural tendency. When a daughter, a famous cardiologist, does open-heart surgery to her own father, her fingers shiver out of fear and her body perspires a lot. You may dishonour your white-hair and order No.1 hair-dye in e-store. To your ill-fortune, a signature mis-match in your cheque leaf brings to limelight that you are growing old. An affectionate grand-father, when he became ill, his grandson turned a blind-eye towards him. He has totally forgotten that it is this grand-father who taught him to ride a bicycle. The pathetic and worst-case scenario is, when the grandfather kicked the bucket, the grandson committed his last rites through a three letter word by texting as "RIP" in Whatsapp. Is the emotions becoming impotent in man, an order of the day. The same grand-father and grand-mother gave him shelter, nurtured him with good food and water when his dad & mom met with a tragic car accident when he was hardly 3 years old, when they left the earth. His maternal uncle who got annoyed of his behaviour, ringed him several times to ask him when will he come and visit his grandparents home. Alas, he texted a message to him. To his surprise, he received a reply 'ASAP'. What sort of happiness he is going to gain by being as a rock of Gibraltor.

I invite you all, to have a joyful journey inside this 'A mystic marionette' what I believed, I sowed and reaped this fruitful book for you all. To err is human, so anywhere in your travel something discomforts you, kindly pardon me. I bow my head to you all.

Bid adieu ....

See you all soon ....

With loads of love,
Aravind

What made me to write

From my childhood days onwards, I had a thirst to write whatever I admire the most. Whenever, I step aside out of my home, I used to carry a piece of paper and a pen. If I get attracted to something, say a rose flower, I will start sketching about the beauty of a rose flower. Since, thoughts donot stay for a longer time and would vanish away, in that worst scenario, paper and pen is the defense mechanism. It is absolutely a God's gift. When I hold a pen in my hand and words flow automatically on its own accord, since it is the will of the God. The thirst for writing grew in gargantuan size everyday and I intensely searched for the source to quench my devilish thirst. I started posting questions in the Science & Technology column, published by The Hindu Newspaper, every week on Thursday's, in the Know your English Q & A column, etc; To add another feather to my thirsty cap, I started posting articles on social issues in "Vent your anger" column, in the Deccan Chronicle Newspaper.

Hitting the nail straight to one's head, if you ask me who is your inspiration in the art of writing, I will utter without any forethought and blindly, **William Shakespeare**. Is there anyday bygone without ruminating the cud of rhetorical phrases "**You too brutus" , "The Daniel has come to judgement", "Sans teeth, sans eyes, sans taste, sans everything in the seven ages of man.** Immersing the heart in the ocean of Shakespeare gives me immense pleasure. Secondly, it is none other than the **God of Small Things author**, **the women of wisdom Arundathi Roy.**

When a beautiful rose is cajoling to the eyes; words flow rhythmically on their own authority, spontaneously. The pen starts scribbling which is underneath :-

I delight in your beauty,
My heart melted in insanity,
To my soul you beget prosperity,

My beloved flower, I get animosity,
When you fade and vanish
From my sight without any pity...

It is sometimes merriment, joyfulness, heart-melting circumstances, memories which invigorates me to write. On the contrary, turning on the other side of the coin, it is annoyment, anger which boils in the blood gets exposed in a paper in the form of words. A man eating biscuits and throwing the wrapper on the road, nullifying the use of dust-bin, urinating by the commonman in the public shamelessly, parents who avoid using their own or public lavatories and making their children to sit on the roadsides for open defecation, a green grocer who is so greedy devising a plan to artificially ripen his mangoes using calcium carbide and thereby reaps profits within a short period, a funeral function which hinders the traffic with pyrotechnic crackers, big garlands thrown up in the procession, which in turn gets hang in electric wires, manual scavenging which is obnoxious to human health and the helpless manual scavengers without any protective cover cleaning the septic tank in the apartments, etc; To the lock, stock and the barrel, the aforesaid examples are only a tip of an iceberg.

Back to the square one, a question strucks in everyone's cerebellum. It is all fine, such unidentified flaw do exists in every society. If that is the case, who is going to bell the cat?

To cut the Gordian knot, whenever I spot such a flaw, which is a deadblock in our growing society, to address the issue, I will be posting my letter in Reader's Mail Column, The Hindu Newspaper. Once again, the bullet will be triggered, is it enough posting a mail to the Newspaper. Who is going to read it and what changes it will make in curbing the malice, and bringing about the renaissances and reformations in the society? I accept my defeat that such maladies do exists in our society for so many decades and it is a hard nut to crack. But like a

Squirrel which helped Lord Aanjaneya to build a bridge which gave the greatest prop & support to the Lord to travel to Lanka, I had adopted this miniscule means, to put up my deliberate efforts dreaming for the renaissance, revival to happen.

Indeed, it is not once in a blue moon, it is several times, so many issues have gone to the ears of the Corporation dignitaries and they had taken necessary action against these social issues and the system got cleansed, purified without any contamination.

In the recent past, Haikus have haunted me in my dreams. The curiosity to colour the Haiku stringently abiding to the rule of 5-7-5 syllables, is everybody's cup of cake and I too is a victim of it. Henceforth, substantially I has started to relish in the world of Haikus. To pick out few from my memories :-

1.Searched light
In a dark room
A blindman's effort...

2.Untamed waves
Loves a single lady
Named as shore...

Yesterday is a dead falcon. Tomorrow is a bottomless mirage. The leftover is today. So, live in the present with joy and happiness in abundance my dear friends. Love you all.

{Aravind Krishnappa Rao}

A Mystic Marionette

1. The dazzling diamonds lost its sheen, when it admired the pebbles which sat disciplined in the tender hands of the children.
2. Eureka! Eureka! In a shrivelling voice, a cute girl shouted on the banks of a river, when she discovered pearls. The gala moment reminded me of Archimedes principle.
3. My pleasing heart is in ecstacy when I ride you. When I get isolated from you, the resultant outcome is broken-hearted. That sweet culprit is a rented bicycle.
4. He is also a biological mother. A horticulturist who obtained labour pain, when he witnessed his arable land getting transmogrified into a shadless desert.
5. Do not anchor the freedom of a child if it intends to float a paper-boat, when it rains cats and dogs.
6. A fathomless fear surmounted a pair of sandals that, they might get lost somewhere. They stood at attention rather than at ease in temple premises waiting for the wearer's arrival.
7. A delicious pasta cooked by mom acutely halted an Ideological war that took place between father and son.
8. Grandpa's migraine got slightly mitigated, when his grand-daughter gave a featherly touch with her palm and rubbed on his forehead. **What a Midas touch it was?**
9. What has been thrown up did not fall down. Is it a plot of Newton's law? My mind wavered hither and thither. The conspiracy got aborted. What has

been thrown up is, an acid in my face. The lotus-like face got blackened by heat, Sir Isaac Newton.

10. The oldage which was kept in clandestine came to lime light by the signature mis-match in the cheque leaf.
11. The hidden animosity behind your enemy's smile is an authentic arsenic poison.
12. The plaintiff, a dead-born-child gave a plaint in the graveyard of Julius Ceaser who laid the foundation for 'C' Section operation. The reasonable complaint is against money swindlers who through their sugar-coated words cajoles pregnant women to opt for ceasarian thereby annuling normal delivery.
13. A squirrel ran steadfast in a cable-wire. A cute girl walked in a rope with utmost dedication and determination. Both the duo, squirrel and cute girl gave me a moral boost that **"courage travels in a straight line."**
14. Mischieviousness of optical illusion. An abandoned goat was saturated with fear, when it looked at a scarecrow in an agricultural land.
15. A cat's-eye stone, which is one of the nine gems, lost its sheen and seemed penniless before an inland letter, which came from my close companion during school annual holidays.
16. As an absent-minded professor, I went in urgency in my motor-bike to attend my uncle's funeral. A voice echoed from a distance, Sir! Please take your side-stand. The soulful voice prevented me from fatality.
17. Electrocution did not occur. Prosecution was not filed in the tribunal. By grasping precisely, the movement of electrons, black sparrow sat on a single electric-wire.

18. You might have won laurels by hiding your Sins. But a rustic drug named prick of conscience corrodes your veins and strangulates your neck every day.
19. The road was intensely unkempt with the spill-over of garbage. It is an unidentified flaw which happens routinely. A closed net over the garbage could have solved this fallacy.
20. The dirty linen was washed in a pious river. Spotless tears oozed out of the salmon fish. Bubbles from the abstergent soap is the antagonist which caused the burning sensation in its eyes.
21. The fruit vendor is so greedy. In order to reap quicker profits he artificially ripened the mangoes. The calcium carbide stone is the sorcerer which did that magic.
22. A civet cat glanced hither and thither to cross the road. Out of crass ignorance, my dunce mind had a suspicion that it is a bad omen which will hinder my work.
23. Chided the crow at a priest and abandoned the lump of cooked rice offered by him. Whenever it sat on a parapet wall, it spotted him rebuking his septuagenarian mother pin-pointing her old-age illness.
24. A chef of a multi-cuisine restaurant glanced his eyes amorously at a boy in the roadside, when he ate emblic myrobalan (Nellikkai in Tamil language) drank some water, rejoiced in its taste and felt as if he is in the seventh heaven.
25. A banyan tree gave its space with humility for an advertisement board. The unbearable pain caused by the hitted nails on its hardcore goes blind to human eyes.

26. Before the advent of inverter, hurricane lamp united the individual souls, who were at nook and corner of the house, to sit together and share their unalloyed happiness with everyone unpretentiously.
27. Cultivate an attitude of gratitude in your life which will help you to shift your thinking towards optimism.
28. An earthworm stood aloof out of starvation as the soil has lost its fertility and land became irreclaimable.
29. **Racism committed self-suicide,** when it glanced at the black and white balloons tied together and stood gigantically in a mobile show room.
30. She woke me up from my slumber impromptu, whispered the river, when rain outpoured at midnight.
31. A basil plant became bashful and felt ashamed when a corrupted palm poured water into the pot.
32. A stubborn beggar with his agnus-eyed vision looked at a devotee, whether the 100 rupees note in his hand, will fall inside the collection box (hundial) or in his begging bowl.
33. A pregnant serpent fought tooth and nail with the mongoose to safeguard its sibling, so that, it can see the sun which is going to rise tomorrow.
34. The perverted intelligence of the boy reached the pinnacle, when he placed his dad's signature in the school report card which carried his meagre marks.
35. The reverberation that followed my nephew's shout, inside a cavern (a large cave) caused discomfort to the bats.
36. A person who spoils other people mirth quite-often gave an ostentatious lecture on the topic "How to be joyful in life".
37. The flare up of street lights even after the dawn represented the polite indifference of Electricity Board staff towards his employer.

38. Is it a breach of trust? Bamboozled the tenant by not paying the rent right from the day of occupancy. He lives at liberty and has no retirement from his active service. He declares his name as house-lizard.

39. On the day of conjunction of the sun and the moon, **firefly acted as a night lamp for the sleeping trees at night.**

40. A back-biter never makes an attempt to look at dirt glued on the back of his body.

41. Is somebody thinking of me? When a milch cow got hiccup it made a guess like this. But, it was a false guess. The candid reason for fuss is, when it gazed in a meadow, a plastic bag got struck on its Larynx.

42. To file an FIR (First Information Report) is meaningless. Performing post-mortem examination is pointless. A tadpole was murdered in a hairpin bend by a vulcanized tyre of a lorry.

43. Right from the antiquated days, a fable which is put forth by an anonymous person's imagination is, in a drum-stick tree there resides an evil-spirit.

44. A hoarded treasure for a boy in a Hamlet is not a chariot or palanquain. Instead of, it is an old cycle tyre and a bamboo stick with luminous dreams in his pupil, he drives this wagon to a star.

45. When I was cutting my nails, my wavering mind got dumbstruck on seeing an ant dragging the nail forward and, all of a sudden, a batallion of ants assembled and transported the nails to their kingdom.

46. Self-hypnotize yourself, before someone hypnotize you and make you clueless in their route-map.

47. An old man lamented in his easy-chair. **You are so selfish selfie**. You might add a better pixilation, but to cut a sorry figure, you do not cover all the members in my joint family, as family photos taken by old cameras.

48. A cloned sheep strived for colostrum (or) beestings. Science has become myopic before the cornea of **Mother's milk which is an ambrosia in ultimatum.**

49. When I bargained with a green grocer tete-a-tete for soaring price of vegetables, the war of words prolonged for few minutes. Alas, when the brawl came to halt, he gave corriander and curry leaves as freebies.

50. On one twelfth day after full moon, Grandpa's demise took place. Bewailed the Grandma by beating in her breast, as they both lived like Anril or crouncha bird, a bird which is said to be inseparable from its mate. When I tried to console her, a 3 letter WhatsApp message came from her Grandson **"R.I.P."**

51. Misdeeds done to others by you, is like a missile boomarang which swings back at you sine die.

52. Whether it is praise (or) censure do not take it to your medulla oblongata and leave it at your sandals.

53. A sudden clash of thunder fluttered the ear-drum of a sheep, when she admired her beauty in a stagnant rain water.

54. Water-hyacinth remorsed at a dried lake which turned out to be a gymkhana for playing cricket.

55. The attribute of kusa grass to bend upon during floods and straighten later on, **stripped off my superfluous ego to nudity.**

56. In front of butcher's shop, with a suspended tongue, stood stray dogs. Apparently, an uninvited guests they are.

57. The modern civilization has a wrong inference that Flora and Fauna are e-waste.

58. Literally, Lavatory is an ideal place, where you can sit relaxedly and get answers for your legitimate questions all of a sudden.

59. During the dog days or the hottest days of summer water crisis, an unlearnt lesson is watershed management. Correspondingly, a learnt lesson is how to lie with statistics.
60. A Foppish boy had a bizzare dream that when starbucks came to India from U.S.A. it sipped Kumbakonam degree coffee.
61. My close friend's beacon of love transferred very swiftly, when he passed his stick to me in the relay race.
62. An hackneyed phrase which is uttered quite often by every father to his son is, you are unfit even for grazing buffaloes.
63. Childhood memories ran amuck in the wave of thoughts. In the Doppler effect, I made the necessary changes. The frequency of waves ran at a snail's pace.
64. A mother's single vow to a deity is, there should exist a harmonious relationship between her cantankerous (or) quarrelsome sons.
65. Although they sat in serenity for meditation, a burgeoning question which ran in the sub-conscious mind of husband and wife is, gender of foetus.
66. **A big pumpkin is a good Samirtan.** To cast away evil-eye's placed on the newly wedded couple, she voluntarily allowed her to brake into pieces.
67. Inspite of myraid number of slaps received, there is no sign of weep and wean. Immaculate waves dashing on the rocks.
68. A boy has not done any mischief. He stood before a noteworthy textile shop and sold kerchief. He virtually made cardinal declaration that survival is absolutely vital.
69. Wherever I wend through during nights, I suspect you follow me. A crescent moon in the blue sky.
70. As the anchor is to the ship, discretion, the ability to find out the right thing, is the axle to the wheel of life.

71. A burning effigy prayed piously to prometheus, Greek god for Fire, to soothen the outrage of the unruly mob.
72. It blossomed after twelve years with perpetual perseverance, a Kurinji flower (in Tamil language) botanically known as strobilanthes kunthiana. In a state of concealment it conveyed patience is phenomenal.
73. What has fallen on a motorist head is not a hailstorm. A passenger from a window seat of city bus spitted betel nut on motorist head.
74. **A buzzing spinning top makes the heart to overflow with joy**. It has a morbid fear on seeing the online games that it might become extinct one day.
75. For a Sunday lunch she cooked delicious vegetable Biryani, Paneer Tikka, Gobi 65 (Cauliflower Fry) and Raita. Her husband and children went in the seventh heaven after eating the sumptuous meal. Alas, as a law of elimination, what is left over for her is curd rice. The mother ate it and went to kitchen for dish-washing the utensils.
76. Children were given smart phones by their parents as a defense mechanism to put an halt to their strange fight.
77. In a pedalled bicycle, a grand-father picks and drops his grandson in the school. Even at his oldage, **he does this labour with absolute civility.**
78. Winged white-ants swarm around the tube-light. They foretell in advance that rain is about to pour.
79. If the Government demonetize, that is okay. If the value of rupee depreciates against the dollar, that too is okay. A stereotyped reply from a city bus conductor is, "I have no change sir".
80. It does not know why? It does not know whether it is the antagonist or protagonist, who has done this? Before getting delivered to a cool-drink shop, large mass of ice got severe blow inside a sac-cloth.

81. A deceiver places falsehood one over another in many storeyed layers without being exhausted. It is similar to a false ceiling placed on a roof-top.

82. My octagenerian grandmother is not at all a qualified ENT (ear, nose and throat) specialist. Through her ages of wisdom, she gave me a virtuous advice, which is, Do not bite the cloth. You will get a stuttering (or) Stammering speech.

83. His friends teased and gave him a pinch at his hind part. They made a mockery at him and shouted clamorously as post-box, post-box. A hole in his trouser taught him a neat lesson that **"Poverty is a man-made hole."**

84. The death knell was beaten to the manual scavenger. Without any protective cover viz; oxygen mask, gloves, he cleaned the septic tank. An innocent human soul was tormented by a poisonous gas. His dead body floated obviously.

85. Whatever stress, migraine, weariness, the populace undergo, it appeases to some extent. It is impartial towards upper strata, bourgeois class and downtrodden. **Idiomatically, a coffee with fine blended chicory is everyone's cup of tea.**

86. I roamed like a live-stock to buy medicines from pillar to post. Each and every druggist gave parliamentary or decent reply as "No stock". Due to dullness of my intellect, later I understood that prescribed medicines are solely and exclusively available in the hospital pharmacy.

87. There is no need to fill any application form. Admission process is relatively zero. Age is not at all a constraint. **A railway platform allows people of all ages to practise walking exercise.**

88. Inspite of her awards, recognitions, a renowned cardiologist, when she did open-heart surgery to her beloved father, she perspired out of fear and her

fingers trembled. The outcome of Electra-complex (excessive love towards a father and hatred towards a mother) in a girl.

89. Children do not maintain safety-locker facility with any nationalised or private sector banks. When the well was dredged, the workers confiscated golden chain hidden under alluvial sediments.
90. The ancestors were so hungry. During the season of water scarcity, a grandson went helter-skelter in search of water in the river, in the lake, holding in his hand a ball of cooked rice to be offered to the manes.
91. A monopolized LED (Light-emitting diode) light bulb, gave its farewell and said bid adieu to halogen lamp with a distressed note written as hey! tungsten, light from yellow bulb could not be seen any more.
92. When a nickel coin was thrown inside a temple bank, it stirred up in the water by making a tinkling sound and got amalgamated with the copper coin who are his ancestors.
93. In a hot mid-day, when the march-past took place, a poor boy stood in solitude as his blue strap (or) war in hawaii slipper was torn-off. In a formless state, **Sir Walter Hunt gave his helping hand through his invention of safety-pin.**
94. An old man was punished although he had not committed any crime. His innocence got rewarded, when a manja kite fell from a branch of banyan tree and sickled his neck while cycling.
95. Hero worship in a teenager has crossed the line of demarcation. He skipped an important appointment given by gastroenterologist to his septuagenarian father, to see first-day first-show (FDFS) of his celebrity movie.
96. A hen-pecked husband engaged in a chit-chat with his colleague on the jargon inflationary pressure, GDP, repo-rate, monetary policy. Suddenly, his termagant wife interrupted and roared, air-conditioner got malfunctional

proximo. Till now, you hadn't ringed to electrician and got it reparied. At this juncture, you are very much worried about our economy.

97. Two decades ago, a stingy fellow was caught red-handed by the Railway Ticket Supervisor for not carrying with him platform ticket. A boisterous laughter bursted when his friends saw him. One among them shouted, hey miser! If you had bought platform ticket by spending 10 rs., you could have saved the fine amount of Rs.300/- Aren't you aware of the economics behind this?
98. The deity from Sanctum Sanctorum came to see the uncontaminated smile in a child's face in the cradle and sang lullaby in its ears.
99. She is not the Member of Parliament, not the member of Legislative Assembly, not the CEO of a top. IT firm who has been admitted in the ICU. **It is our own mother planet who is in ICU**. Although she has got sufficient oxygen support, she has a million-dollar question and doubt that whether the next generation will support her.
100. A falcon gave a clarion call towards an old hag, **'You are a mystic marionette'.** You never know the truth and all through your winters, you hadn't taken any efforts to know what is truth? You simply dance according to the tune of others. You are a puppet activated by others. Notabene, you are a mystic marionette.

THE END.

www.ingramcontent.com/pod-product-compliance
Lightning Source LLC
LaVergne TN
LVHW070226170826
845679LV00034B/1857

9798896322368